Groundbreaking

Innovative Practices in Urban Agriculture

Table of Contents

Chapter 1. Introduction

Urban agriculture, once a niche pursuit for eco-conscious city dwellers, has now become a groundbreaking tool in the global fight against food insecurity and climate change. Its innovative practices are rewriting rules and transforming our city landscapes, making them greener, healthier, and self-revolving. This Special Report on "Groundbreaking: Innovative Practices in Urban Agriculture" dives into the heart of this revolution, exploring cutting-edge techniques, success stories from around the world, and what this means for our future. With accessible language and an upbeat approach, we journey through rooftop gardens, vertical farms, community greenhouses, and innovative tech that are not only reshaping our cities but also offering solutions to some of our most pressing environmental issues. Every page is a discovery, making this report an absolute must-have for anyone interested in sustainable living, fresh food, and the future of urban design. Don't miss your chance to be part of this green revolution, grab your copy today!

Chapter 2. The Rise of Urban Agriculture: A History and Overview

The recognition of urban agriculture as a significant contributor to sustainability and a means to combat food insecurity has been a gradual yet transformative process. While only in recent years has it gained mainstream attention, the practice has a long history that tracks back to the very beginning of city settlements. Today, it's making its presence felt in our urban landscapes through rooftop gardens, vertical farms, community greenhouses, and more. Understanding the history and evolution of urban agriculture provides invaluable insights as we stand on the brink of what many are calling the 'green revolution.'

2.1. The Beginning: Ancient Civilizations and Agriculture

Urban agriculture is by no means a new concept. Ancient civilizations, such as Mesopotamia, Egypt, and Pre-Columbian America, provide evidence of farming within city boundaries. They utilized innovative means to deliver water to crops, employed various soil management techniques, and even dabbled in 'vertical farming.' The agricultural surplus produced by these societies allowed for increased specialization, population growth, and the development of early urban environments. Though not labelled 'urban agriculture,' the rudiments of the practice were firmly embedded in these city settlements.

2.2. The Industrial Revolution and City Farms

Fast forward to the industrial revolution. The revolutionary technologies led to rapid urbanization in Europe and North America. People flocked from rural areas to cities, seeking job opportunities. This movement resulted in a new urban class with no access to rural farmlands. Some turned to city farming out of necessity, transforming vacant lots into cropland and raising livestock within the urban setting as a means to supplement their diet and income. Despite this, there was still a distinct divide with farming regarded primarily as a rural industry.

2.3. The Emergence of Victory Gardens

The value of urban agriculture was further recognized during the world wars. Confronted with food shortages and rationing, citizens across the United States, Canada, United Kingdom, and Australia were encouraged to start 'victory gardens.' People cultivated fruit, vegetables, and herbs in private yards, rooftops, empty lots, and even city parks. During World War II, it's estimated that these victory gardens produced as much as 40% of all the vegetable produce consumed in America.

2.4. Post War Decline and Resurgence

Post-war prosperity in Western nations led to a decline in urban gardening, replaced by large-scale factory farming methods that promised quick and convenient food production. However, as environmental and health impacts of industrial agriculture started becoming evident, there was a resurgence in urban farming in the 1970s and 1980s. During this time, an increasing emphasis was placed on sustainable living and greener cities.

In the developing world, urban agriculture never really collapsed but continued to play a crucial role in providing food for urban dwellers and underserved communities. In many African and Asian cities, urban farming was a means of survival.

2.5. The Urban Agriculture Revolution of Today

Today, there's a profound recognition of urban agriculture's potential to address multiple modern challenges. Technological advancements, changes in consumer preferences, and a raised awareness of climate change, food security, and the need for sustainable practices, have put a new spin on this age-old practice. The rise of the eco-conscious consumer, coupled with the technological advancements, is pushing urban farming to the forefront of sustainable development.

2.5.1. Vertical Farming

Space constraints in urban areas brought upon an innovative solution - vertical farming. Multi-story greenhouses, such as New York's Sky Vegetables, are maximizing yields using a fraction of the space required by traditional farms. These controlled environments enable year-round production of a variety of crops, despite the outside weather conditions.

2.5.2. Rooftop Gardening

Space maximization doesn't stop at vertical farming. Urban dwellers have been harnessing the potential of empty rooftops to create urban oases, providing green space and food production in densely populated cities. In Montreal, an entire industry has evolved with companies such as The Green Line: Green Roof, actively converting urban rooftops into sustainable vegetable gardens.

2.5.3. High-tech Urban Agriculture

High-tech approaches are marrying computer science with agriculture to augment urban farming. Hydroponics, aquaponics, and aeroponics are systems that don't rely on soil, opening up possibilities for where food can be grown. Additionally, we're witnessing the use of sophisticated climate control technologies, robotics, and artificial intelligence to optimize plant growth, nutrient content, and yield within these systems.

2.5.4. Community Gardens

The growth of community gardens has also become an essential urban farming trend. These shared green spaces provide not only fresh produce but also contribute to social cohesion, recreational activities, and community building. They can be seen in cities worldwide, from Sydney to London, New York to Tokyo.

Urban agriculture, from its ancient roots to its modern iterations, has been a resilient and resourceful response to the demands and challenges of urban living. It is now emerging as a viable and innovative solution to contemporary issues of climate change, food security, and sustainability. As we move further into the 21st century, we can only expect its influence and presence in our cities to grow. The urban agriculture revolution is not just a trend; it's a way of life, a crucial part of urban development taking our cities towards a greener, healthier future.

Chapter 3. Revolutionary Spaces: Rooftops and Balconies as Green Havens

As cities worldwide continue to expand, the conventional notion that agriculture belongs solely to rural areas is being turned on its head. Innovative urban dwellers see potential where many only see concrete and glass - rooftops and balconies.

Rooftops and balconies are unconventional lots for cultivating plants, becoming the most unlikely green spaces. They bring transformative power, injecting life into otherwise dormant and underutilized areas, ensuring agriculture continues to grow even in dense urban centers.

3.1. Understanding Space Optimisation: The Promise of Unused Rooftops

City expansions are often associated with squeezing out nature and agriculture. However, practitioners of urban agriculture see rooftops as underutilized assets waiting to be unlocked. Let's walk through the creative process involved in transforming unused rooftops.

Initially, a structural assessment is necessary to determine whether the building can support the weight of a rooftop garden. Once cleared, the process can proceed. Roof sealants are installed to prevent potential leaks, followed by a layer of insulation and a waterproof membrane. Raised garden beds or hydroponic systems are then introduced, depending on the urban farmers' preference.

This setup not only enables the growth of crops but also provides certain environmental benefits. It improves air quality and reduces the "urban heat island" effect, where concrete and asphalt absorb more heat, making cities hotter. Hence, rooftop gardens not only utilize space; they contribute directly to mitigating climate change amidst dense urbanization.

3.2. Balcony Gardening: From Barren Corners to Lush Sanctuaries

Similar to rooftops, balconies are an embodiment of using every available square meter for urban agriculture. Seen as opportunities instead of limitations, balconies shine as small but potent spaces for plant cultivation.

The first step involves assessing what can grow successfully in terms of sunlight exposure, heating, and wind conditions. One common approach is container gardening, where plants are grown in pots or other containers. This method is ideal because it offers portability and the chance to customize soil mixtures for different plant types. Vertical gardening is also prevalent, especially for small balconies, like using trellises and tiered planters to maximize space.

Growing plants on balconies not only provides fresh produce but also fosters mental wellbeing. Caring for plants induces tranquility, and when your balcony brims with vegetation, it creates an instant escape, a sanctuary amidst the city's hustle.

3.3. Innovative Techniques Pushing Boundaries

Innovations are rapidly transforming rooftop and balcony gardening. For instance, hydroponics—where plants are grown without soil—reduces the need for heavy soil beds, ideal for rooftops and balconies. Another technique is aeroponics, where plants are grown in air or mist environments without the use of soil or an aggregate medium. This method is efficient in terms of water and nutrient usage.

Automated systems leveraging technology are also on the rise. They allow busy urban dwellers to manage their rooftop or balcony gardens remotely, ensuring optimal results with less manual labor. Such technologies help broaden the appeal of urban agriculture, accommodating busy city dwellers who may have been deterred otherwise.

3.4. Green Success Stories from Around the World

Multi-story buildings and high-rises aren't barriers to plowing and planting. Examples of successful transformation of rooftops and balconies into green havens are emerging worldwide.

In Singapore, the densely-populated city-state, "SkyGreens" is a vertical farm that employs a hydraulic water-driven system to rotate vegetable troughs. This innovative method allows for 10 times more yield per unit area than conventional ground-level farming. Meanwhile, in New York City, "Brooklyn Grange" operates the world's largest rooftop soil farms, spanning across two roofs in Brooklyn and one in Queens. They grow over 50,000 lbs of organically-cultivated produce each year.

These success stories are powerful testaments to urban agriculture's potential and the changing tides towards eco-conscious city living.

3.5. Today's Green Havens: Tomorrow's Blueprints for Sustainable Cities?

Urban agriculture's emergence indicates a pivotal shift in how we perceive and use city spaces. By repurposing unused rooftops and balconies into lush, productive green havens, we actively contribute to a paradigm shift towards sustainable urban living.

Rooftop and balcony gardens, though small in individual scale, can have a monumental collective effect. They reconnect urbanites with nature, reduce carbon emissions, provide local food sources, and enhance biodiversity within city limits. They challenge conventional farming narratives and promote sustainable lifestyles that could be a significant part of the solution to current environmental issues.

The revolution is not on the horizon—it's already here, on our rooftops and balconies. As we march towards greener pastures, let's carry the mantra: If you can't find green around, create it — and not just on the ground. These underused, underappreciated areas hold the seed for a greener, brighter future, turning our cities not just into concrete jungles, but into urban ecosystems that nourish both people and the environment.

As we gaze from our skyscrapers or walk down our busy streets, let's marvel at the sprouting seedlings, the fruit-laden trees, and the smiles of urban farmers. Up above, down below, in every corner and balcony, therein lies the heartbeat of our cities - incessantly growing, always greener.

Chapter 4. Towers of Life: The Science and Implementation of Vertical Farming

Vertical farming, a futuristic concept that has matured into a possible solution for a sustainable future, stands as an awe-inspiring spectacle amidst modern urban landscapes. Transcending the space constraints, it breathes life into skyscrapers and warehouses, transforming them into vibrant green spaces – towers packed with layers of edible life.

4.1. The Science of Vertical Farming

The root idea of vertical farming capitalizes on optimizing space, allowing crops to grow vertically indoors, in contrast to traditional farming's sprawling horizontal acreage. But vertical farming isn't simply stacking soil beds one above another; it's an intricate system infusing several sophisticated technologies.

Hydroponics and aeroponics form the crux of vertical farming. Hydroponics revolves around cultivating plants in water-based, nutrient-rich solutions instead of soil. It enables the root system's direct contact with essential nutrients, leading to fast growth rates. Aeroponics, on the other hand, employs the tactic of hanging plants in the air, feeding them by misting nutrients onto the roots. This process optimizes oxygen absorption, promoting healthy plant development.

Another cornerstone technology is Controlled Environment Agriculture (CEA). CEA involves growing plants within an artificially controlled environment – monitoring and adjusting variables like light, temperature, humidity, and CO2 levels to attain optimal plant growth conditions year-round.

Artificial lighting, using LED lights, plays a crucial role in vertical farming. These lights are calibrated to emit specific wavelengths, harnessing the spectrum most beneficial to plant photosynthesis. This narrow spectrum application uses less energy and does not radiate heat, thereby enhancing efficiency and productivity.

4.2. Successful Innovations and Implementations

The skyline of cities across the globe is gradually becoming greener owing to various successful implementations of vertical farming.

In Singapore, a city-state with minimal arable land, Sky Greens has pioneered low-carbon hydraulic water-driven, tropical vegetable urban vertical farming. Sky Greens' A-Go-Gro towers have significantly accelerated vegetable growth, providing local, sustainable produce to the residents.

Chicago's The Plant, an old meatpacking warehouse turned vertical farm, houses diverse businesses including a brewery, a bakery, and aquaponic growers. Its closed-loop system capitalizes on waste heat and output from one business to fuel others, demonstrating an ecosystem that thrives on sustainable symbiotic relationships.

Across the Atlantic, Europe's largest vertical farm in the Netherlands, GrowWise, is a dynamic hub of research and development. In collaboration with Philips, it's developing and testing various LED light recipes to optimize different plant species' growth.

Farm.One, based in New York, follows a niche approach cultivating rare and exotic herbs, edible flowers, and microgreens. Shying away from mass-crop production, it underscores vertical farming's potential as a provider of diverse, gourmet, locally grown, fresh produce.

4.3. Vertical Farming and Sustainability

Vertical farming emerges as a solution to the pressing challenges of traditional farming – land and water scarcity, use of fertilizers and pesticides, and climatic uncertainties.

Being enclosed environments, vertical farms use up to 95% less water than conventional farming, as the circulated water can be recaptured and reused. Further, it negates the need for pesticides, as a controlled environment curbs pest infestation, ensuring cleaner, healthier produce.

In the context of space efficiency, vertical farms pound for pound outperform their conventional counterparts. A study reveals that a 30-story vertical farm could potentially produce the same yield as a 2,400-acre traditional farm.

Moreover, the indoor nature of vertical farming neutralizes the unpredictability of weather, making possible year-round production and fostering food security in regions facing severe climatical constraints.

4.4. Challenges and the Road Ahead

Despite the robust potential, vertical farming must navigate a set of challenges. High establishment and operational costs often limit its viability. Electricity, infrastructure, and technology costs far outweigh traditional farming investments.

Furthermore, vertical farms currently focus on growing quick-yielding leafy greens and herbs. Cultivating staple crops like wheat, rice, and corn, with their lengthy growth period and extensive root system, is infeasible in this system.

However, continuous technological advancements and economies of scale are gradually driving down costs. Energy-efficient LED technologies and automation are progressively making the vertical farming model more viable.

Ultimately, vertical farming is more than just an architectural spectacle; it's a framework for agriculture of the future – promising high yields, preserving resources, mitigating climate change, and nudging us towards a sustainable future Cityscape. As our cities grow, so will our buildings, and in them – our farms, creating true towers of life. Despite the challenges, the promise of a greener, healthier, and sustainable urban future proffers immense opportunities - an invitation to push the frontiers of what is possible with vertical farming.

Chapter 5. Harnessing Technology: Hydroponics and Aquaponics in Urban Settings

5.1. Understanding Hydroponics and Aquaponics

Hydroponics is a type of gardening that uses no soil, but instead grows plants in a solution of water and nutrients. A hydroponic system can grow plants and vegetables faster and year-round. The system is set up to allow the plants to take up only what they need for growth, hence energy is conserved, and the plants grow more efficiently.

Aquaponics, on the other hand, is a symbiotic system uniting aquaculture and hydroponics. Fish or other water-dwelling creatures are grown in a tank, and waste from those creatures is used to feed hydroponic plants. The plants remove nutrients from the water which, in turn, purifies the water for the fish. This creates a closed-loop system where resources are constantly recycled, mimicking natural ecosystems.

5.2. Advancements in Hydroponic Technologies

With continuous improvements in synthetic nutrient solutions and complex nutrient timing systems, hydroponics has evolved beyond a simple water culture into a viable method for large-scale, year-round produce farming. New technologies, including efficient LED lighting systems and sealed greenhouses, have significantly reduced the energy required for hydroponic farming, making it even more sustainable.

A fascinating development in hydroponics technologies is the rise of automation. Today's hydroponic farms can feature automated nutrient delivery and pH balancing systems, automatically adjustable lighting, and remote monitoring and control of the hydroponic systems via smartphones. These advancements not only simplify the farming process but also further enhance the efficiency and effectiveness of crop cultivation, making the method an even more attractive prospect for urban settings.

Another notable development is the use of vertical farming techniques in hydroponics. Vertical farming stacks hydroponic systems vertically, allowing a great number of plants to be grown in a relatively small space.

5.3. The Evolution of Aquaponics and its Potential in Urban Agriculture

Aquaponics, while not as widely used as hydroponics, has great potential in urban agriculture due to its efficiency and sustainability. It combines the versatility and high yield of hydroponics with the natural nutrient cycle provided by aquaculture, which saves resources while providing both fresh vegetables and a source of protein.

The synergy created in an aquaponic system leverages the natural processes that occur in each subsystem, leading to gains in efficiency that neither system could achieve alone. Innovations in this space include the utilization of solid waste from fish tanks to create vermicompost – providing a source of necessary micronutrients for the plants – and the increased use of renewable energy systems for powering the setup.

5.4. Implementing Hydroponics and Aquaponics in Urban Agriculture

While the use of these systems in rural and commercial agriculture has a relatively long history, their application within the context of urban agriculture is a newer phenomenon. Urban environments provide unique challenges including limited space and often lack of natural sunlight. However, smart incorporation of these methods into the urban environment can offer many benefits.

Indoor hydroponic gardens, for example, can be fit into almost any space, making them a great solution for city residents with limited outdoor areas. They can be set up inside living rooms, on balconies, or in basements.

Similarly, aquaponic systems require less land and water than traditional agriculture, making them well suited to urban environments where access to these resources may be restricted. Aquaponics also has the added benefit of producing not just plants but also fish, providing a source of protein that can be difficult to access in some urban environments.

5.5. Succeeding with Hydroponics and Aquaponics: Case Studies

Several cities around the world are leading the charge in deploying hydroponics and aquaponics on a large scale. In Sundbyberg, a suburb of Stockholm, a 3,000 square meter rooftop has been converted into a commercial hydroponic farm. Here, a variety of crops are grown in specially designed pods that help insulate plants in winter and cool them in summer. Vertical farming techniques allow this rooftop farm to produce the equivalent of 2000 acres of conventional farming annually.

Take an example of aquaponics from Milwaukee, Wisconsin in the United States. Sweet Water Organics, an urban aquaponic company, transformed an old factory into a fish and vegetable farm. Using fish waste as fertilizer, the company produced Swiss chard, watercress, and other vegetables, while also raising tilapia.

Both of these case studies demonstrate the potential for hydroponics and aquaponics to transform urban areas into productive landscapes while addressing issues related to food security and sustainability.

=== Taking Urban Agriculture to the Next Level

Hydroponics and Aquaponics provide us with the tools we need to reimagine our cities and to build food systems that not only provide fresh, local produce, but that also help to build community, promote wellness, and address many of our most pressing environmental concerns. They are more than simply 'next-gen' farming techniques – they represent a new way of thinking about how we feed our urban populations, and a new vision of what our cities can and should look like. Innovative use of these techniques represents the vanguard of urban living design, a way for us, as a society, to combine the best of urban and rural lifestyles, creating a healthier, more sustainable future for us all.

Certainly, there are challenges to popularizing these systems, particularly concerning initial set up cost and technical knowledge required. However, as the technology and techniques continue to advance and become more accessible, we can expect to see a rise in urban agriculture systems around the globe. We're on the cusp of a green revolution in urban living, and hydroponics and aquaponics are leading the charge.

Chapter 6. The Power of Community: Neighborhood Gardens and Greenhouses

In any urban landscape, you'll find an intersection — a crossroads where humankind and nature coexist. In more recent years, there's been an influx of green in these concrete jungles, a testament to our collective yearning for a connection with the Earth. Enter neighborhood gardens and greenhouses, the modern urbanite's foray into sustainable agriculture.

6.1. Harnessing Local Potential: The Birth of Community Gardening

Community gardening isn't a new concept. In fact, its roots extend deep into our history, sprouting during times of crisis when food was scarce. Today, these gardens are much more than just a source of sustenance; they're an embodiment of unity, collective responsibility, and environment-conscious living.

So, what changed? As our cities grew, so did our disconnection with nature. The once clear demarcation between rural and urban blurred, giving rise to a unique fusion: urban agriculture. Neighborhood gardens sprouted amidst high-rises and bustling streets, tapping into local resources and thriving off shared enthusiasm.

6.2. Reinvigorating Spaces and Communities

These community gardens and greenhouses have shown immense

potential in transforming idle urban spaces into lush, green, productive sanctuaries. They offer a unique perspective on space utilization in densely populated cityscapes, replacing concrete eyesores with verdant oases.

They also foster a strong sense of community. Neighbors, who barely interacted, now toil together in shared plots. Elderly citizens, looking for constructive ways to occupy their time, now find purpose in nurturing saplings. Children, playing on screens indoors, now play in the mud and learn about the circle of life firsthand. Community gardens bring people together over a shared ecosystem that thrives on collaborative effort.

6.3. A Gateway to Food Security

Food security is a complex issue that countless people across the globe encounter. In a world where 690 million people still go hungry, urban agriculture proposes an audacious solution. The idea is simple: grow your food locally, reducing dependence on imported goods and mitigating food scarcity.

Food grown in community gardens is typically organic, free from pesticides, and often much fresher than store-bought produce. It's a small but significant step towards achieving food sovereignty at a local level, paving way for healthier and more sustainable choices.

6.4. The Role of Community Greenhouses

Community greenhouses are essentially an upgrade to traditional community gardens. They offer controlled environments to grow a variety of produce that wouldn't typically survive in a city's climate. Often using innovative technology, these greenhouses can maintain specific conditions for growth and yield a more diverse produce selection. It means fresh tomatoes in winter or leafy greens in the scorching summer, redefining seasonality in food production.

These greenhouses also double as learning centers, offering workshops on how to cultivate different types of produce. This hands-on education not only imparts valuable skills but also kindles a deeper understanding of what it takes to grow the food we eat.

6.5. The Environmental Impact

Community gardens and greenhouses help counter many urban environmental issues. They work as carbon sinks, reducing the overall carbon footprint, and improve air quality by eliminating pollutants. In bustling cities where asphalt and concrete amplify heat, these green spaces act as coolants, mitigating the urban heat island effect.

Moreover, these spaces also promote biodiversity, inviting a variety of insects, birds, and other species, strengthening the urban ecosystem. They can also reduce waste by encouraging composting, turning kitchen scraps and yard waste into nutrient-rich soil.

6.6. Challenges and Solutions

Despite the phenomenal advantages, establishing and maintaining community gardens and greenhouses possess unique challenges. These range from issues with land tenure and gardening skills, to accessibility and funding. However, with robust community involvement, public and private support, and innovative problem-solving, these challenges can be successfully navigated.

6.7. A Vision for Our Urban Future

The power of community gardens and greenhouses extends far

beyond their immediate tangible benefits. They are tools of resilience and empowerment, teaching us the value of self-sufficiency and cooperation. They show us that concrete megastructures and lush green spaces can coexist and that our cities can become more than just places of dwelling – they can become thriving ecosystems.

As we move towards an uncertain future with climatic changes looming large, these community-centric practices serve as an ark, holding the promise of a more sustainable, resilient, and environmentally conscious urban life. Our relationship with food, the environment, and each other is changing, and these urban agricultural practices are leading the charge towards a greener future.

The adventure of community gardens and greenhouses has just begun, and everyone is invited. Let's sow the seeds of change together. Urban agriculture is not just a trend; it is shaping up as a social revolution that promises to redefine our relationships with cities, food, and each other. By localizing food production, we are taking a significant step towards a more sustainable, healthy, and inclusive urban life.

Chapter 7. Edible Landscaping: Cultivating Beauty and Nutrition

As the city wakes up to the hum of traffic and its landscape dominated by concrete structures, there is a quiet revolution taking place. There is a noticeable shift towards integrating food cultivation into the urban environment - a trend known as edible landscaping.

===The Concept of Edible Landscaping

Edible landscaping, or foodscaping, is a practice that merges the utility of traditional farming with the aesthetic appeal of ornamental plants. It replaces non-edible plants in decorative landscapes with crops, fruits, vegetables, and herbs. The idea here is to design planting schemes that contribute to the city's beauty and also its plate.

The scope of edible landscapes is vast; it can incorporate fruit and nut trees, vegetable beds, berry bushes, edible flowers, and herbs into the urban environment. These landscapes can range from vegetable patches in small front yards to wide-scale public installations in parks or along roadways. Edible landscaping not only champions urban food production but also the greening of urban areas, contributing to environmental sustainability.

===The Benefits of Edible Landscaping

Edible landscaping offers numerous advantages. Firstly, the ability to grow food in an urban setting empowers city dwellers to take charge of their nutrition intake. Such an approach also encourages healthier eating habits as residents have easy access to fresh, organically grown produce.

In addition to these health benefits, edible landscapes are more environmentally friendly than traditional gardens. They increase green spaces and biodiversity in the city, improving air quality and reducing urban heat effects. Here are some key benefits of edible landscaping.

1. **Food Security**: Enables localized food production, decreasing dependence on food import chains.

2. **Health**: Provides access to fresh, nutritious, and chemical-free food.

3. **Environment**: Increases green spaces, promotes biodiversity, and contributes to carbon sequestration.

===Designing an Edible Landscape

Designing an edible landscape requires a shift in mindset from traditional gardening. It calls for creative integration of edible plants into a design that enhances the aesthetic appeal of the space. Designing tools such as layering, focal points, harmonious plant combinations, and use of color can be instrumental in creating effective layouts. For instance, a purple cabbage can offer attractive ground cover with an added bonus of a healthy harvest.

Plants in edible landscapes should be chosen based on their adaptability to local conditions, their resistance to pests and diseases, and their nutritional value. It's also essential to consider the aesthetics, including the plant's size, shape, texture, and color.

===Edible Landscaping Around the World

From individual households to public parks, the concept of edible landscaping transcends geographical boundaries. Cities across the world showcase different interpretations of this green revolution, each with its own unique context and challenges.

In Todmorden, England, 'Incredible Edible' has transformed public spaces into vibrant vegetable gardens while beautifying the township. In France, the town of Albi aims to be self-sufficient by 2020. Indeed, in Havana, Cuba, gardened rooftops and balconies provide an impressive 90% of the city's fresh produce.

===The Future of Edible Landscaping

Edible landscaping has the potential to redefine our cities radically. As urban agricultural practices gain further traction, we can expect to see more green spaces, reduction in food miles, and healthier citizens who have a direct relationship with their food.

However, for such a vision to materialize, urban planners, horticulturists, and the broader citizenry need to actively participate in and support edible landscaping initiatives. Such collaboration will ensure that the movement of edible landscaping transforms from a quiet revolution to a mainstream urban policy.

In conclusion, edible landscaping holds great promise for the future of urban design and planning. This innovative approach not only encourages healthier lifestyles and community bonding but also answers to pressing environmental and food security issues.

Chapter 8. Composting in the City: Closing the Loop on Waste

Urban composting is a necessity in taking a stride towards sustainable urban living, turning waste into a resource and fully embodying the principles of a circular economy. The process involves organic waste decomposition into nutrient-rich soil, simultaneously reducing the need for synthetic fertilizers and confronting the issue of food waste.

8.1. Urban Composting: Turning Waste into Wealth

Around 40% of municipal waste is organic, which primarily comes from food. When discarded, this waste contributes to greenhouse gas emissions in landfills. However, this waste isn't waste - it's a misplaced resource that, rechanneled, can rejuvenate soil fertility and reduce pollution. Composting at the city scale possesses the potential to turn this organic waste into environmental wealth.

Composting involves the breakdown of organic matter by microbes under controlled conditions. They consume organic waste and excrete nutrient-rich compost (humus) as a by-product. This compost can rehydrate soil, save water, enhance aeration, support microorganism biodiversity, and provide plants with the required nutrients.

8.2. Implementing Urban Composting

Composting in an urban setting can be established in various forms: individual composting, community composting, and city-wide composting. Individual composting, the simplest form, typically comprises households managing their organic waste. Compost heaps or boxes are used to compost kitchen waste and garden trimmings.

Community composting involves residents of a specified area or members of an organization collectively composting their organic waste. This model is often observed in urban community gardens or schools.

In city-wide composting, municipal authorities collect, segregate and compost organic waste. This compost is utilized in public parks or sold to farmers and gardeners. Several cities globally, including Seattle and San Francisco, have implemented successful city-wide composting systems.

8.3. Techniques and Technologies for Urban Composting

A variety of composting methods can be adopted, each tailored to handle different types of organic waste, space requirements, and user commitment. Here are few examples:

1+|===

|^|Traditional Composting ^|Bokashi ^|Vermiculture ^|Aerated (Turned) Windrow Composting ^|In-vessel Composting | Overview |Mix green and brown waste in a heap, turn periodically.|Mix waste with a group of microorganisms and leave it in a sealed container.|Red worms eat organic waste and produce nutrient-rich compost.|Large volume of organic waste is formed into windrows

(long rows) and aerated mechanically.|Organic waste is composted within a drum or silo. | Waste type |Yard and kitchen waste.|All kinds of kitchen waste.|Only raw fruit and vegetable scraps.|High volume of green waste.|Food waste from kitchen, hospitality, or post-consumer. | Space |Small to large.|Small.|Small.|Large.|Medium. | Time|Few months.|Few weeks.|Few months.|Few weeks.|Few weeks. | Level of effort|Medium.|Low.|Medium.|High.|Low. | Compost quality|Good.|Very good.|Excellent.|Good.|Very good. ===

8.4. Success Stories: Turning Trash to Treasure

San Francisco, a city on the world stage, was the first to require city-wide composting in 2009. Their comprehensive program has successfully diverted 80% of waste from landfills, towards the goal of zero waste by 2020.

In 2015, New York City launched a composting program, reaching 3.5 million residents and processing over 46,000 tons of organic material annually. The compost is used to enrich soil in urban farms, community gardens, street tree pits, and park landscapes.

8.5. Urban Composting and the Future City

An urban composting revolution can fundamentally change the way we manage waste, transform landscapes, and approach food systems. People become closed-loop citizens, actively contributing to healthier soils, growing fresh local food, and reducing waste pollution.

Substantial progress is being made across the globe in the realm of urban composting. However, challenges around regulations, logistics, and public participation still persist; they need addressing to scale these models.

But, as citizens increasingly see waste as a misplaced resource and cities as potential hubs of composting, we inch closer to a future of greener, healthier, and circular cities. Urban composting, in such a vision, is not just an act, but an assertion of sustainable urban existence.

In conclusion, composting in the city, closing the loop on waste, paves the path towards a regenerative urban future. It is a simple yet profound act - taking what is unwanted, turning it, and returning it enriched, renewing the urban soil to yield healthy crops and sustainable lifestyles.

Chapter 9. City Bees, City Trees: Urban Biodiversity and Why it Matters

In the world of concrete and high-rise buildings, not many people pause to consider the critters that cohabitate with us. Urban biodiversity has often been overlooked, given our nature to separate 'nature' from our 'urban' environments. However, recent scientific evidence suggests that urban environments can and do support a wide range of flora and fauna. The inevitable hint: city-dwelling bees and trees, integral components of urban biodiversity, have been playing a significant role in our cities.

9.1. The Concrete Jungle: Home to More Than Just Humans

Skyscrapers, bridges, and city parks aren't only for humans navigating the busy cityscape; many species of flora and fauna coexist with us within the urban matrix. City parks and small green spaces often serve as wildlife oases, providing crucial habitat for birds, insects, and various mammals. One might spot a rabbit scampering through the undergrowth, or a hawk circling high above in search of prey.

Believe it or not, urban areas often support a surprising array of insect life. Chief among these are bees, whose crucial role in our ecosystems cannot be overstated. As pollinators, bees play a vital part in the web of life, ensuring successful reproduction for a myriad of plants. It is estimated that one out of every three bites of food we eat is thanks to a pollinator.

A city need not be devoid of trees either. Urban forestry, the practice of managing trees within an urban environment, has gained significant traction in recent years. Trees are more than just aesthetically pleasing additions to our cities—it's their ecological role that adds a unique value.

9.2. Bees in the City: Urban Apiculture

Urban apiculture, or beekeeping, has grown in popularity over the past decade. Urban beekeepers cultivate hives on city rooftops, balconies, and in backyards. It might sound strange, but cities can be ideal environments for bees. Urban green spaces, gardens, and street trees can provide diverse sources of pollen and nectar throughout the growing season. Plus, urban environments usually lack the agricultural pesticides found in rural areas, benefitting the overall health of the bee population.

Paradoxically, some research suggests that urban bees are more productive than their rural counterparts. This might be due to a greater diversity of plants in urban areas. Furthermore, urban heat islands—pockets of cities that retain heat—extend the growing season, providing bees with a longer window to gather resources.

9.3. A Forest in the City: Importance of Urban Trees

The benefits of urban trees are manifold. They store large amounts of carbon, helping to mitigate climate change. Through transpiration and providing shade, trees also have a cooling effect, counteracting urban heat island effects and thereby reducing energy consumption by decreasing the need for cooling systems during warm months. Besides, trees absorb air pollutants, thus contributing to cleaner air and healthier urban populations.

Urban trees also encourage biodiversity by providing food and shelter for a variety of bird species and pollinators. A good diversity of trees, shrubs, and ground-cover plants can create a wide range of habitats for these critters to inhabit.

However, successful urban forestry requires careful planning and management. Species must be carefully selected for wakefulness to local climatic conditions, tolerance to pests and diseases, and their ability to tolerate the urban environment's challenges, including air pollution and limited root space.

9.4. Challenges and Solutions to Urban Biodiversity

While bees and trees undoubtedly add to the biodiversity of cities, they also face many challenges. Bees can suffer from lack of habitat and exposure to pesticides, despite lower levels than in agricultural areas. Urban trees, on the other hand, often face restrictive growth conditions due to soil compaction and limited space, which can inhibit their life spans and overall health.

However, innovative solutions are being established to enhance urban biodiversity. For instance, 'green roofs'—roofs covered with vegetation—as well as city parks are being promoted as potential bee habitats, while the concept of tree-lined streets and urban green corridors is being explored for urban forestry.

Species-specific initiatives are also a powerful tool in enhancing biodiversity in our cities. Consider the "Bee City" movement which encourages communities to pledge to create sustainable habitats for bees. Similar efforts are being made with urban forestry, like the Urban Tree Canopy (UTC) initiative aimed at enhancing tree cover in urban environments.

In conclusion, urban spaces have great potential for supporting biodiversity—it's just a matter of recognizing that potential and taking the necessary steps to support it. The booming popularity of urban apiculture, along with the increased interest in urban forestry, marks a positive trend towards cities embracing their natural aspects, transforming from concrete jungles to thriving urban ecosystems.

Chapter 10. Global Success Stories: Case Studies in Urban Agriculture

Urban agriculture has exploded in popularity across the globe, with urban farming innovations cropping up in cities large and small. The following case studies provide a deep dive into some of the most successful urban agriculture projects worldwide. Each paints a unique picture of how innovative agricultural practices can be adapted to urban environments, battling food insecurity, promoting community engagement, and offering sustainability benefits.

10.1. Detroit, USA – Turning Blight into Bounty

In Detroit, urban agriculture has been a beacon of hope, confronting urban blight and a food desert head-on. The city hosts more than 1,500 community gardens, thanks to the backing of organizations like Keep Growing Detroit which promotes food sovereignty by empowering urban gardeners and other local businesses.

The Detroit Black Community Food Security Network runs D-Town Farm, a seven-acre organic farm that provides food, job training, and educational programming. Equally inspiring, the Michigan Urban Farming Initiative runs a fully functional urban agrihood, offering food free of cost to around 2,000 households within two square miles.

Detroit's urban agriculture movement is proof that urban farming can fill in where traditional commercial food systems fall short, and can even help stimulate economic growth and urban renewal.

10.2. Havana, Cuba – An Urban Farming Revolution

The island nation of Cuba, especially in its capital city of Havana, is a case study in the power of necessity driving invention. After the collapse of the Soviet Union in the '90s, the Cuban food supply was devastated. The response was a nation-wide shift towards self-sustaining organic urban farming, also known as 'organopónicos'.

Former industrial sites have been converted to gardens, producing a wide variety of vegetables to supply the city's population. It's estimated that urban agriculture supplies about 60-70% of all the fresh vegetables consumed in Havana.

10.3. Todmorden, United Kingdom – Incredible Edible Town

Todmorden, a small town in England, pioneered the concept of turning public spaces into food gardens. Incredible Edible Todmorden started as a local movement, aiming to build stronger communities and enable local food production.

From corn grown outside the police station to apple trees in the railway station car park, the local community now actively participates in growing and harvesting food. The project has sparked widespread interest and similar initiatives are cropping up across the globe.

10.4. Tokyo, Japan – Pasona Urban Farm

Urban agriculture in dense urban areas often requires thinking vertically. This ideology is embodied by Pasona Urban Farm. Located in Tokyo's busy business district, this nine-story office facility incorporates an innovative urban farm right into the building.

More than 200 species of plants, including fruits, vegetables, and rice are grown using a combination of hydroponic and soil-based farming. The farming systems are integrated throughout the building in atriums, walls, rooftops, and even underground.

Plants not only provide local fresh produce but also help control climate within the building and offer employees a refreshing green environment, blending agriculture with corporate life in an unprecedented way.

10.5. Singapore – A Model for High-Tech Vertical Farming

Singapore is a major innovator in vertical farming technology. With limited land and a high demand for local produce, the city-state is uniquely motivated to maximize farming efficiency.

Sky Greens is a pioneering vertical farm that grows vegetables in rotation on nine-meter-tall towers. Using hydraulic-driven technology, the system rotates the plants for even sunlight distribution and utilizes gravity to assist in irrigation. It uses less water, less land, significantly reduces food miles and produce can reach consumers within 24 hours of being harvested. It's a true testament of the potential of vertical farming in an urban context.

Each of these inspiring examples paints a unique picture of how urban agriculture is being applied worldwide. These holistic and innovative approaches may pave the way for more cities to creatively incorporate green solutions, inspiring self-sustainability and healthier communities. With dedicated efforts, every concrete jungle has the potential to breathe easier and offer its inhabitants the joy of freshly cultivated produce.

Chapter 11. Looking Forward: Future Trends and Predictions in Urban Farming

Urban agriculture is not just a phenomenon, but a promising future that unlocks new avenues and outlines pathways to achieve food security, promote sustainable livelihoods, reduce carbon footprint, and provide enterprise opportunities. The coming decades will witness drastic transformations in the urban farming sector as it leverages technology, sustainability practices, and social innovations to establish a resilient food system.

11.1. The Technology Leap

Urban farming and technology fall hand in hand. The proliferation of cutting-edge technology has led to sophisticated farming practices which, when compounded with the sustainability offered by urban agriculture, signals towards a future replete with extensive productive cityscapes.

A shining star in the technological banquet is precision farming. Big data, IoT (Internet of Things), and automated systems are playing pivotal roles in moving urban farming from an interest of the eco-conscious to an established, efficient choice for city dwellers. Predictive analytics tools, based on these technologies, enable farmers to anticipate both shortcomings and excesses in conditions that affect plant growth, enhancing crop planning and harvest-related decisions.

Vertical farming is emerging as an effective way to bring farming within the confines of urban spaces. By growing in stacked layers, this practice makes optimum use of available cubic space instead of surface area. Controlled Environment Agriculture (CEA) techniques regulate factors such as temperature, CO2, humidity, and light, catalyzing photosynthesis production rates for year-round crop production, independent of external weather conditions. Complemented by hydroponic systems, vertical farms drastically reduce water usage, making them an eco-friendly, sustainable solution.

Emerging technologies like gene editing and advanced sensors promise new horizons in urban farming by optimising growth conditions tailored for each plant and increasing resistance to diseases and pests – all while reducing the use of chemical fertilizers and pesticides.

11.2. The Sustainability Shift

Mindful urban famers are consistently grappling with an essential question: "How can we produce more with less?". The answer lies in sustainability. The future of urban farming is intrinsically tied to sustainable management of resources, be it water, energy, or waste.

Facing an imminent threat of water shortage, modern urban farms have adopted innovative methods like rainwater harvesting and use of greywater systems. Farms that utilize water from such non-traditional sources minimize dependence on existing potable water, showing a viable path towards maximal utilization with minimal waste.

In the energy sphere, renewable energy sources such as wind, hydro, and solar power are replacing conventional techniques. By harnessing these renewable energy sources, urban farms are mitigating climate change, enhancing food security and supporting green jobs, without compromising yield or safety.

Furthermore, urban farms are partaking in a global "zero waste" movement. Organic waste generated in the city is quickly converted into nutrient-rich compost for urban farms. This lowers methane emissions from landfill waste while maintaining soil fertility and reducing the need for chemical fertilizers.

11.3. The Social Impact

Urban farming integrates physical activity, nutrition education, and social connection into one cohesive package, consequently impacting community health and cohesion. City dwellers reconnect with food origins, illuminating gaps in the existing food system and encouraging healthier diets and lifestyles. Simultaneously, urban agriculture promotes social inclusion by creating shared spaces that encourage community interaction and foster a collective sense of responsibility.

An aspect often overlooked is the role of urban farming in urban planning and its impact on the built environment. Increasingly, urban spaces are being designed to incorporate farming infrastructure. Green roofs, vertical farms, aquaponic systems, and more are becoming integral elements in modern architecture and city landscapes, reflecting the shift towards a more integrative model of urban planning.

11.4. Predictions and Trends

In the wake of these transformations, several exciting trends are foreseeable. Automation is expected to move from luxury to the norm in urban farms, with smart systems managing water and nutrient supply. Simultaneously, decentralized food supply chains featuring farmer's markets, cooperatives, and direct-to-consumer models will pave the way towards local food sovereignty.

Looming large is the vision of smart cities designed around sustainable food systems. Here, urban agriculture will not be an afterthought, but a driving force dictating building designs, energy systems, and waste management. In essence, our cities will evolve into active food producers rather than mere consumers.

Incorporating urban farming into climate resilience strategies is garnering attention. Urban farms can act as green lungs, helping cool down pronounced urban heat islands and increasing soil sequestration of carbon, making cities more resilient.

The future of urban farms is indeed promising. But to attain this future, commitment from all stakeholders—from municipal policymakers to urban dweller—is imperative. Proper regulations should be put in place to promote urban farming and make it viable for both farmers and consumers. Jointly we can ensure that urban agriculture will forever shift the narrative of food production, becoming an essential component of the fabric of urban life.